17
f
21
ff
25
mf
29

33
37
ff
41
45
mf
f

Early Advanced Piano Solo

Celebration Scherzo

Martha Mier

Alfred

Alfred's PREMIER PIANO solos

Dedicated to the Hattiesburg Music Teachers League of Hattiesburg, Mississippi in honor of their 2001 Composer Festival

Celebration Scherzo

Allegro (♩ = 138)

Martha Mier

49
mp
53
f
57
mp
mf
61
ff

65
mp
mf
69
73
f
77

81
85
mp
88
91
ff
(no rit.)
fff

Alfred's

RECITAL SUITE SERIES was created for performing piano students. Each suite is a short collection of fresh-sounding solos carefully crafted to be played as a group in a recital. Musical challenges, appropriate for the level, provide interest and appeal. Aspiring pianists are challenged to reach higher degrees of excellence while playing music that is truly enjoyable for them and their audiences.

Martha Mier's

Florida Reflections, in three movements, showcases the seasides and waterways of one of America's leading tourist states. See the water sparkle and hear the waves splash in *Treasures from the Sea* while searching for seashells along a sandy beach. Take a trip to *The Everglades* through the lush harmonies of the music and experience this vast marsh that covers much of South Florida. *The Suwanee River* features the Florida State Song, "Old Folks at Home." Beginning slowly and freely, this movement builds to a rousing ragtime finale that will leave the audience humming and tapping their feet.

Intermediate (22394)

Marilynn Ham's

Michigan Images paints a musical picture of three of the natural and man-made wonders of this state. Each movement features a distinct style and landmark. In *Mackinac Bridge Overture*, the great expanse of the world's longest suspension bridge is depicted by stately chordal passages and sweeping melodic lines. The irresistible driving rhythms of the '60s Motown Sound is found in *Motown Mix*, which also uses the mixolydian mode. *Many Moods of the Great Lakes* shows the shimmer and sparkle of a perfectly calm lake as well as the tempestuous storms that can rage across the water. As a whole, the suite creates a canvas of many moods and colors for both the listener and the performer.

Late Intermediate to Early Advanced (22392)

Peter Jancewicz's

Sketches of Canada takes the pianist on a sweeping tour of this impressive country. The four movements are written in different styles and represent many of the Canadian provinces. *Misty Canadian Mornings* evokes daybreak over Algonquin Park in Toronto, Ontario and the ancient cedar forests in British Columbia. Travel to the East Coast and experience the Maritime Provinces in *Fisherman's Shanty*, a movement that incorporates two famous folk songs from the area. *Prairie Hymn* visits the Prairie Provinces and is a musical picture of their wide, open spaces. The suite is brought to a thrilling conclusion with *Carnaval de Québec*, a tribute to one of Canada's most famous festivals, the Quebec Winter Carnival.

Late Intermediate to Early Advanced (22393)

Other titles available in Alfred's *Recital Suite Series:*

Arkansas Suite
Martha Mier
Intermediate (20781)

California Coastline
Tom Gerou
Late Intermediate (21321)

Mississippi Moods
Catherine Rollin
Intermediate (21397)

An Australian Journal
Tom Gerou
Intermediate (21410)

The Lone Star State
Gayle Kowalchyk
Intermediate (22427)

New England Memories
Gayle Kowalchyk
Intermediate (21322)

Alfred Publishing Co., Inc.
16320 Roscoe Blvd., Suite 100
P.O. Box 10003
Van Nuys, CA 91410-0003
alfred.com

9780739020869
TP
APEX

SINDING

RUSTLES OF SPRING Op. 32, No. 3

EDITED BY MAURICE HINSON

AN ALFRED MASTERWORK EDITION

Alfred

Biography of Christian Sinding

Christian Sinding was born on January 11, 1856, in Kongsbreg, Norway, and died in Oslo on December 3, 1941. This celebrated Norwegian composer studied first with L. Lindeman in Norway, then at the Leipzig Conservatory with Schradieck (violin), Jadassohn (theory), and Reinecke (orchestration); after four years (1877–81) he returned to Norway, where his piano quartet and a symphony were performed in Oslo. A government income enabled him to continue his studies in Germany, and he spent two years (1882–84) in Munich, Berlin, and Dresden; there he wrote his first opera, *Titandros*, much influenced by Wagner. In Germany, he published a number of piano pieces in salon style and of these, the *Rustles of Spring* became an international favorite. He was invited by George Eastman to teach at the Eastman School of Music in Rochester, New York, during the academic season 1921–22. After this journey, he lived mainly in Oslo and continued to compose. Toward the end of his life he wrote in larger forms. His third symphony was conducted by Nikisch with the Berlin Philharmonic in 1921, and his fourth symphony was performed on his 80th birthday in Oslo in 1936. Most of his music is of a descriptive nature; his lyric pieces for piano and his songs are fine examples of Scandinavian Romanticism, although the German inspiration of his formative years is much in evidence. He was greatly influenced by Robert Schumann and Franz Liszt. Sinding's music is less nationalistic than Grieg's although he is regarded as the latter's peer in many respects by some authorities.

Performing "Rustles of Spring"

Sinding is best known in the United States by this charming salon piece. In northern Europe spring arrives very suddenly, the snow melts quickly, the meadows become green all at once, the songs of birds, like the river, burst forth in full flood, and once again the "long and dreary winter" is forgotten as we look forward to the warmth of summer. Just as the rustling silk skirts of a lady's dress in approaching a room announce her coming, so too before spring arrives there seems a curious lull in Mother Nature, as though she yawns before awakening; there is a rustling in the air just before we can say "Spring is here!" Perhaps this resembles the picture Sinding has in mind when he composed this attractive composition.

From experience I find few young pianists able to perform this piece in time, and therefore I recommend strict, liberal use of the metronome. Many students grumble and object to the metronome, but until you can keep strict time with the four basic 8ths in the measure (at a slow pace), you will never be quite sure of the other relative rhythmic values. And this uncertainty will quickly ruin the effect of this piece.